C000115810

by
J. B. Midgley

*All booklets are published thanks to the
generous support of the members of the
Catholic Truth Society*

CATHOLIC TRUTH SOCIETY
PUBLISHERS TO THE HOLY SEE

Contents

Acknowledgements

The CTS gratefully acknowledges recourse to the following sources: Vie de Saint Dominique, Henri Lacordaire OP, Paris 1840; Life in Mediaeval England, J.J.Bagley, Batsford, London 1960; Oxford Dictionary of Saints, D. Farmer, Oxford University Press, Oxford 1978; Christian Monasticism, D. Knowles OSB, Weidenfeld & Nicolson, London 1969; The Papacy, P. Johnson, Weidenfeld & Nicolson, London 1997; Saint Dominic, S. Tugwell OP, Editions du Signe, Strasbourg 1995; The Mind and Heart of St John Baptist De La Salle, Tr. E. Bannon FSC, LaSallia-Oxford 1997; Life of Saint Dominic, B. Jarrett OP, Burns Oates & Washbourne, London 1934; The English Dominicans, B.Jarrett Op Burns Oates & Washbourn, London 1937; The Jerusalem Bible, Darton, Longman & Todd, London 1974. The Divine Office, Collins, London 1974; The Westminster Hymnal, Burns Oates & Washbourne, London 1948; The Stripping of the Altars, E.Duffy, Yale University Press, 1992.

Preaching the Gospel in Europe

What kind of a Europe was Dominic born into? By the end of the twelfth century, it was a Europe that had made considerable economic, civil and political progress. Ecclesiastical revival of spiritual and institutional health had been accompanied by developments in scholarship, science and the arts. The Church had re-established her authority under the pragmatic and wise leadership of Pope Innocent III (1108-1216) who took rulers to task if they dared interfere in clerical appointments for political advantage, and is remembered by the English for releasing them from their allegiance to King John. However, such advances had not yet helped the Faith of those who now dwelt in expanding towns and cities. The parish system was largely rural, and parish priests had difficulty in taking adequate care of the urban, often impoverished laity. Into such a world God sent the Friars, (Fr, frères, or brothers) who followed two remarkable men in changing the face of mediaeval Christianity.

Francis and Dominic

In Italy, the layman Francis of Assisi saw a need for preachers and, with apostolic zeal, preached penance and the wonder of Christ's saving mercy, calling on all to turn away from sin to praise, love and serve God. The ordained and learned Dominic in Spain had the wider vision of an organised religious order that would announce the mysteries of God's Kingdom, answer Our Lord's call to make disciples of all nations, teach them to observe His commands, reveal the truths of the Faith, and correct departures from that truth. Both men gathered followers to preach the Gospel in the highways and byways, care for the poor and oppressed, develop the homily as a parochial feature, call people to follow Christ, teach them the Christian Faith, and combat heresy. Their Friars described themselves as mendicant because they owned nothing, relied on alms for their subsistence, and accepted the most basic place to sleep.

The Franciscans and Dominicans won the confirmation of the Holy See in 1210 and 1216 respectively. They cherished poverty in a search for spiritual riches that outshines preoccupation with earthly goods, and dedicated their lives to Christ who advised taking "nothing for the journey, neither staff nor haversack, nor bread, nor money, nor even a spare coat and footwear." Like the monks, they were devoted to liturgical worship, but their separation from the world differed from that of the monastery as they combined contemplation with social activity. To the Orders of Friars, Pope Innocent IV added the Carmelites in 1245, and Pope Alexander IV the Augustinian Hermits in 1245, so that Chaucer, in his '*Prologue to the Canterbury Tales*' around 1390, can speak of "alle the orders foure." (cf. *Mt* 10:9, 28:20; *Lk* 9:3).

How the orders were organised

The Founders of the monastic orders had taken it for granted that each monastery would be independent under the direction and care of the Abbot. Francis had no particular organisational structure in mind for his followers, and Dominic founded a "religious order" in the way the description is now understood. He adopted the Rule of St Augustine that could be modified without neglecting the fundamental commitment to poverty, prayer and study. As it transpired, the community unit would be the Convent led by a chapter of members who elected the Prior, or "first brother". Priors and elected delegates would meet in a Provincial Chapter that voted for a Prior Provincial and Council, and Priors Provincial and delegates would meet in General Chapter, and be entitled to elect the Master-General and his Council. Administration would be through Provinces that contribute to the General Chapter, and the Provincial and General Chapters as legislative bodies acting through Priors Provincial and a Master-General elected by and accountable to these assemblies. The Master General was later retitled 'Master'.

In time, the First Order of priests and brothers extended to a Second Order of contemplative nuns, and a Third Order Regular of conventual sisters who teach, nurse, and serve in domestic and foreign missions. There is also a Third Order Secular for diocesan priests and members of the laity who practice a modified Rule of evangelical life compatible with their responsibilities, and who acknowledge the authority of the Master General, and are guided by a Friar who meets with them regularly for prayer and instruction. It was during his last visit to Lombardy that Dominic founded the Third Order of lay members as the "Militia of Jesus Christ" who would protect the rights and property of the Church and oppose heresy. Distinguished numbers are St Catherine of Siena, St Margaret of Hungary, St Rose of Lima and the Blesseds Columba of Rieti, Ingrid of Sweden and Sybilla of Parva. Today the terms 'First, Second and Third' Orders are not generally used.

Importance of learning

Dominic believed his Friars should be scholars versed in the Scriptures and writings of the early Fathers so that they could bring the Faith to others and correct the departures from orthodoxy that imperil members of Christ's Body. His evangelization was less by moral exhortation and denunciation than by a cultured interpretation of the truths of Faith, the exposition of doctrine, and an accurate explanation of the Catechism. Cardinal Newman observed that as Benedict is the symbol of the retreat of learning into the desert, Dominic is the symbol of its return.

His Friars enjoyed the patronage of successive Popes who valued their ministry in towns and cities as preachers, confessors, and energetic spiritual directors with doctrinal knowledge and pastoral skills to help diocesan clergy. The people noticed that they were faithful to their vows, did not expect tithes or rents, and as mendicants were dependent on alms. Enthusiastic crowds came to hear them preach, and bishops gave the support that renewed religious practice and attracted a steady flow of aspirants to the Order from all levels of society. Some secular clergy even resigned their livings to join them, though some others begrudged the popularity of well-educated rivals.

The destitution of the first Friars was extreme and heroic, but scholars need manuscripts, writing materials, and tolerable places in which to work. Gradually, warmer clothing, adequate food and accommodation were introduced as common-sense necessities. They became renowned teachers in the universities of Europe, and achieved eminence in the flowering of theology and philosophy. The Dominican Thomas Aquinas, was the "Doctor Communis", the "master of all", the greatest thinker and theologian of his and succeeding generations, universally acknowledged as the norm of orthodoxy.

Dominic wanted to experience the truth of God's Word and share with others the news of His universal and constant love and compassion for all His people. He was convinced that he was called to evangelise by his presence in the world and by living a life that reflects the goodness of the Creator. He founded an Order that is truly Apostolic in its emulation of Our Lord who went about the land on foot, preaching to the people, making time for them, being available to His disciples, and gathering disciples to take the Good News to the corners of the earth. Like the Son of Man who had nowhere to lay His head, he relied on the kindness of others for survival and, in confronting the Albigensian theory that God is not yet in total control, he was at one with Isaiah: "How beautiful on the mountains are the feet of one who brings good news, who heralds peace, brings happiness, proclaims salvation, and tells Sion, 'Your God is King'" (*Is* 52:7-8).

'The word you are to preach'

Dominic took to heart what St Paul's said about "a variety of gifts, and the particular way in which the Spirit is given to each person. One may have the gift of preaching with wisdom given by the Spirit; another may have the gift of preaching instruction given by the Spirit" (1 *Co* 12:4-11). He walked Europe's often inhospitable and perilous paths to preach the Gospel and combat heresy with heroic courage and unwavering certainty. He urged all his brethren to "Go without anxiety, because the Lord will give you the word you are to preach, and He will be with you so that you will lack nothing." His last words to them were that he would be more useful to them after his death than when alive. We can be sure that, from his place in heaven, he continues to offer loving and powerful friendship to those who proclaim the Good News of the Kingdom by the way they live, to those given the specific mission to preach the Gospel, and to all who counter contemporary secular undermining of Faith, or reverse self-inflicted dilution of its teaching. When Gospel values and traditions engendered by Christianity come under siege from secular morality, or state legislation seeks to overrule conscience, Saint Dominic will intercede for us and be our eager guide.

St Dominic's Church,
Downham Market, Lent, 2007

Dominic: the formative years

Dominic Guzman was born in 1170 at Calaruega, a small town in the diocese of Osma in Old Castile. The family home was near the Benedictine Abbey of St Dominic of Silos, 1000-1073, a circumstance that may have inspired his parents' choice of name. Felix and Joanna Guzman were of Spanish nobility and, some say, connected to the reigning House of Castile. Felix was the admirable head of an exemplary family, and Joanna led a life of such holiness that Pope Leo XII beatified her in 1826. Before Dominic's birth she is said to have received a vision in which he appeared with a black and white dog that held in its mouth a flaming torch that illuminated the world. The influence of such parents was not lost on Dominic and his two brothers, Antonio and Mannes, who were distinguished for their sanctity. Antonio, the eldest, was ordained to the secular priesthood, distributed a considerable patrimony to the poor, and spent his life ministering to the sick. Mannes followed in Dominic's footsteps, became a Friar Preacher, and was beatified by Pope Gregory XVI not long after his mother, the blessed Joanna.

Education

The young Dominic soon showed signs of earnest piety and a prayerful disposition. He even used to get out of bed to lie on the floor because it was less comfortable, an early practice of self-denial to which Dante referred in the *'Divine Comedy'*. It is not surprising that he was entirely happy with his parents' decision to direct his career towards the Church. At seven, his education began under the guidance of his uncle who was archpriest of Izan near Calaruega. At fourteen, he enrolled in the University of Palencia where, for the next ten years, he was a model student. His determination and dedication gave some the impression that he was solemn and austere, but most tell of his patience, cheerfulness, consideration for others, and radiant energy. He was deeply moved by the sufferings of others that invariably elicited a tender compassion and concern. When famine struck Palencia, he sold his books with priceless annotations to feed the poor commenting, "I do not want to study 'dead skins' while people are dying of hunger." His friend and biographer Bartholomew says that he even offered to go as a slave to Morocco in place of a poor woman's brother who had been seized by the Moors. His generous response to human need of others had an impact on fellow students who followed his example.

The Canon of Osma

In the twelfth century, the monastic "common life" which brothers or sisters share in religious communities became an option for diocesan priests who did not take religious vows. It involves living under the same roof, praying together, taking meals and recreation together, sharing goods and property, and supporting one another in the demands of their vocation. Bishops like St Thomas Becket of Canterbury encouraged a united and reformed Canterbury Chapter to live according to the Rule of St Augustine as Austin, Black, or Regular Canons, and congregations were formed of diocesan priests who embraced community life with a modified monastic rule.

Dominic's studies at Palencia progressed from the arts to theology, and his reputation attracted the attention of the saintly Bishop Martin of Osma who wanted to reform his cathedral Chapter. He believed that Dominic would offer an example of holiness that would help introduce the common life under the Rule of St Augustine, and with Diego de Azevedo, the head of Chapter, invited him to join the Chapter of Osma. Dominic accepted and, according to the early biographers, was ordained in 1195. He was soon entrusted with the senior post of Sacristan, and when Diego succeeded Martin as Bishop in 1201, he became

Prior of the Reformed Chapter of Canons Regular where, for nine years, he led a cloistered life dedicated to the public worship of God, prayer and study. His early biographer, Blessed Friar Jordan of Saxony writing in 1234, describes his life during this period when remarkable gifts of character and personality were revealed:

"He appeared among his brother canons as a bright ray of sunshine, in humility of heart the least, in holiness the first, shedding around him the fragrance of quickening life, like the sweet scent of pine woods in the heat of a summer's day. He frequented the church, ceaselessly devoted to prayer, scarcely venturing beyond the cloister walls, the more to find time for his thoughts with God. He had been given a special grace of being able to pity sinners, for those troubled or afflicted, and the thought of their misery distressed his heart to the point of tears. It was his custom to spend the night in prayer to God with reverent love, and his special petition was that God would give him a true love to be effective in saving souls. Only then could he consider himself a real member of Christ's mystic Body gaining all for whom his Lord Jesus had spent Himself on the Cross."

Missionary zeal

Diego and Dominic were kindred spirits and firm friends. In 1203, when King Alfonso IX of Castile asked the Bishop to help arrange a marriage between his son, Prince Ferdinand and a Danish Princess, daughter of the Lord of the Marches, he took his Prior with him as chaplain. The route and destination of the group of clergy and knights is uncertain, and opinions vary as to whether it went to Denmark or if there was a meeting in France, but a happy settlement was reached. Two years later, they made a similar journey to escort the betrothed to her groom. Some say the Princess was taken ill and died on her way to Castile, others that she decided to enter a convent. Certainly, Diego had to send a message to the King telling him the wedding was off, and that he and Dominic were making a detour to Rome to visit Pope Innocent III. Like Our Lord, Dominic had led a hidden life, and was about to embark on a public ministry with intense energy.

Their travels had taken them through Toulouse where they had seen the spiritual damage being caused by the Albigensian heresy. Perhaps it was then that Dominic began to think about a religious order that would combat error and preach the Gospel to those still waiting to believe. He and Diego also became aware of the ravages wreaked by pagans who had been recruited as mercenaries by warring contenders for the crown in Germany. The Bishop asked Innocent's permission for prolonged leave of absence from his diocese to fulfil a missionary desire to convert the unbelievers, and take the Gospel to the Cumans and Tartars, but the Pope thought the diocese must remain the first priority, and had already decided that the two could help him with the Albigensian problem.

The Albigensian Crusade

The heresy

In the tenth century, a Bulgarian called Bogomil
("beloved of God") had founded a dualist movement
whose members, *"Bogomils"*, came to be generally
described as *"Cathars"* (Greek *"katharos"*, *"pure"*).
Cathari philosophy was based on the "absolute dualism"
of two battling eternal powers, Good-Spirit and Evil-
Matter; and "mitigated dualism" in which the superior
Good-Spirit ultimately prevails over the inferior Evil-
Matter. Albi, a town in Languedoc, gives its name to the
Albigensian approach to dualism, which was influential
in southern France and northern Italy between the twelfth
and fifteenth centuries. It has been described as
cosmological and anthropological in its view of a good
God who created the angels and human souls, and an evil
god, Satan, who made the physical, material world, and
these two battle for the control of the cosmos.

Albigensians believed that human salvation is a
process of alignment with the good God in which the soul
becomes free from the contamination of the flesh. They
therefore recommended severe asceticism, celibacy, and a
fasting so rigorous that it was sometimes fatal. They

rejected marriage because, "to multiply human souls is to multiply damnation," and regarded suicide as the choicest form of death. They refused to bear arms or swear oaths, rejected the Sacraments and the clerical hierarchy, and sought to widen their influence by setting up their own parallel "dioceses" to rival those of the Church. In their own ranks, they distinguished between those who were less "advanced", and "Pure adherents", the "Perfect Souls" who would successfully pass through a cycle of death and reincarnation. The Pure did, however, have a rite in which they initiated others deemed worthy of attaining their own lofty status. Their itinerant preaching won many followers, especially among the poor who admired their renunciation of the world, their condemnation of the rich and powerful, and their pious deportment that unfortunately was not always a characteristic of the clergy.

The Crusade

In 1204, Pope Innocent appointed Abbot Arnaud Almaric of Citeaux, and two other Cistercian monks, Peter of Castelneau and Raoul of Fontfroide, as Papal Legates with a commission to convert heretics in southern France by preaching and, because heresy was a civil crime, to bring the stubborn to justice. Progress was not impressive, and was hampered by the questionable example and reputation of some local clergy. They also had to contend with the active opposition of potentates like Count Raymond of Toulouse who protected the heretics usually for political reasons. The Pope asked Bishop Diego and Dominic to go to Languedoc and see what could be done, and the Canon emerged from the sheltered cloister of Osma as one certain of his vocation, imaginative, courageous, and with a universal vision. He was considerate and affectionate to all with whom he came in contact, and always without a hint of personal ambition.

When they arrived they were sceptical about the efficacy of the Legates' splendid retinue that prompted Dominic to observe, "How can you expect success with all this worldly pomp? These people cannot be touched by words without deeds. Throw away your splendour and go forth like the disciples of old, barefoot and without money, to proclaim the truth." He and Diego led by example, and the legates followed. Other Abbots joined the campaign that for a while was conducted zealously and fruitfully. As the Cistercians had not been enjoying one of their admirable periods, Dominic also took the opportunity of recommending a return to an austere way of life.

Albigensian beliefs were disseminated mainly by theological exposition and debate. Dominic's studies and training at Palencia had equipped him splendidly to answer in kind and, when opponents realised they could not match the quality of his preaching they expressed their animosity by heaping insults on him. He was undeterred by danger, telling those who threatened his life, "I am not worthy of martyrdom. I have not yet merited such a death." His faith and sense of humour protected him in the face of persecution, and John of Saxony remembers that even his enemies whom he never avoided were perplexed, often disarmed by his winning personality. The preaching of Diego and Dominic, and their manifest lack of ostentation and self-interest won many back to the faith, despite the organised support given to the heretics by sections of the clergy, some bishops, and powerful nobles.

Prouille and a moment of grace

On 22nd July 1206, the Feast of St Mary Magdalen, Dominic was on a hill just outside Fanjeaux, prayerfully reflecting on the limited success thus far, and gazing down at Prouille, a small town in the diocese of Toulouse. Here, Our Lady granted him a vision that brought a determination to undertake a great work beyond the confines of Albigensian territory and, surprisingly, make Prouille the centre of his apostolate. From these headquarters, he laboured tirelessly in Fanjeaux, Montpellier, Servian, Beziers, and Carcassonne, and the hill of his vision came to be remembered as "*Signadou*", "*the Sign of God.*"

Dominic establishes his first Convent for nuns

Many women 'Perfects' who actively disseminated Albigensian beliefs formed religious communities that practised asceticism. Parents, especially of the lower nobility, were so impressed that they entrusted their children's education to these articulate and cultured ladies but, in so doing, exposed them to error. Happily, Dominic's charismatic preaching and constant effort brought some of the "Perfects" back to the Faith. Bishop Foulkes of Toulouse, a holy and inspiring prelate, gave him the church of St Mary in Prouille and next to this he arranged basic accommodation for an orthodox convent initially of nine sisters. He gave them a suitably modified version of St Augustine's Rule with appropriate constitutions that demonstrated his conviction that fidelity to the cloister, the example of a holy life, and constant prayer for others to receive the gift of faith were powerful antidotes to heresy.

As an educational establishment, the convent gained such an enviable reputation that by 1207 it was attracting supportive donations, and Dominic later made it the first double convent by providing separate buildings for some of his Friars who helped with the nuns' subsistence. Necessarily brief descriptions of events in Dominic's mission, only underline the astonishing speed at which he brought projects to a confident and successful conclusion.

The importance of Prouille's development in his life and the story of his Order are confirmed by a statement coming from the General Chapter of 1644 held in Rome. "We declare that at Prouille there is not only the monastery of the Nuns of the Order, but also a Priory of Friars Preachers founded by our blessed father, Saint Dominic who was himself its Prior, which Priory has been confirmed by Pontifical Bulls."

Growing religious conflict

Not everything continued smoothly. The civil authorities continued to side with the heretics, the Abbots returned to their monasteries and Cistercian involvement declined. In July 1207, Bishop Diego had to return to his diocese where he died in December, and Dominic was left alone with a tiny spiritual army. Now that it was obvious that the strategy to correct the heresy had failed, Pope Innocent began to think about armed intervention, and his mind was made up early in 1208 when his Legate, Peter of Castelneau, was assassinated probably at the instigation of Count Raymond of Toulouse. Innocent asked Philip II of France to lead a crusade but he refused, no doubt because western rulers were busy resolving differences among themselves. A variegated army of mercenaries, regulars, and fortune hunters was assembled under the command of Simon de Montfort the elder who was an example of Christian chivalry. English history remembers his son Simon Earl of Leicester, as a patriot, statesman, and the pioneer of constitutional rule by his victory over Henry III at the Battle of Lewes.

In the ensuing religious conflict exacerbated by political feuds, Dominic always advocated mercy, "wielding the arms of the Spirit while others wrought death and destruction with the sword." It is said that during the sack of Beziers, he was in the streets, crucifix in hand, pleading with the military for the lives of women, children, the aged and the sick. Some chroniclers doubt his presence there at the time but are universally agreed that such conduct was typical. He and de Montfort became friends, and he followed his troops so that he would be in a position to reconcile heretics in towns and cities that had capitulated, and restore orthodox religious practice. He was at the siege of Lavaur in 1211, at La Penn d'Ajen when it was captured a year later, and at Parmiers where his efforts restored some sense of religion and morality. On 12th September 1213, he attended the council held on the eve of the battle of Muret and the next day, during the fighting, prayed for a Catholic victory. This proved so conclusive that de Montfort gratefully paid for a chapel to be dedicated to Our Lady of the Rosary in the church of St James. Dominic's friendship with de Montfort continued until 1218 when the latter was killed at Toulouse.

Offers of episcopate

Dominic's reputation for sanctity, apostolic zeal, administrative efficiency, profound learning, and sensitive leadership skills brought offers of bishoprics, the last being the see of Navarre in 1215. All were declined, and he said he would rather "take flight in the night with nothing but my staff than accept an ecclesiastical honour." Providence was at work nevertheless, and when the Papal Legate Peter of Benevento, asked him to be head of the preaching mission with headquarters in Toulouse, it was an appointment he could not refuse.

An Order of Preachers

When they started their preaching apostolate in 1204, Dominic and Bishop Diego were helped by some well-disposed men, some of whom were fellow Canons of the Osma Chapter. A few withdrew for a variety of reasons, but those who remained increasingly adopted a religious way of life in makeshift accommodation in Prouille. In the light of this and his vision there, Dominic recognised the advantage of having a group united in a bond stronger than the fluctuating enthusiasm of volunteers, in effect, a religious order dedicated to the correction of heresy and to the propagation of religious truth. Providence was soon at work.

Bishop Foulkes of Toulouse believed in the importance of the parochial system, admired Dominic and saw the value of his preaching mission. He proposed the establishment of a permanent institute with authority to preach in the diocese and recruit new members. He said he could offer them only the basic financial support given to the poor, but invested Dominic with the chaplaincy of Fanjeaux, so that the attached stipend could be used for essential development. In July 1215, he canonically established the religious community as a diocesan congregation for the "teaching of faith and morality and the elimination of heresy." One of the first novices from Toulouse was Peter Seila who, like St Francis, was a rich, young merchant. He owned some houses near the castle of Narbonne that he made available to Dominic for a community residence. On 15th August, the Feast of Our Lady's Assumption, Dominic received the community's first religious profession.

The Friars soon proved their worth as they served the Church through the efficient exercise of a mission, the aims of which they had clearly identified and defined. It was a good start, but Dominic still envisaged a Congregation that would extend its apostolate to all the nations of the earth. It was becoming clear in his mind that he could organise an Order more mobile than the parochial, diocesan model, and he could care for souls with disciplined, dedicated religious who were active, versatile, and independent of local resources and identity. Events would further his intentions.

The Fourth Lateran Council

Pope Innocent called the Council to begin on 15th November 1215. Dominic was still a Canon of Osma, and it was in this dignified capacity that he accompanied Bishop Foulkes to Rome as his theologian. This assembly, regarded as the most important of the Middle Ages, defined Transubstantiation, the doctrine of the Sacraments, and the nature of the three Persons of the Blessed Trinity in one Divine Substance. It also deliberated on "the improvement of morals, the extinction of heresy and the strengthening of the truth." Civil authorities who had become lukewarm in their responsibility to combat heresy, were asked to revive their co-operation.

Because the Council's agenda included Church discipline and authority, it has been mistakenly assumed that it introduced an aspect of the Holy Office referred to as the Inquisition. In fact, it was not until 1230 that Pope Gregory IX in his bull *'Excommunicans'* outlined procedures for identifying heretics in Europe, and even this is sometimes confused with the Spanish Inquisition that was created by Ferdinand and Isabella of Spain in 1481. Certainly, Innocent III had his own tribunal and, in the role of theologian, Dominic would have been asked to judge the orthodoxy or error of an accused person. Only two related documents mention his participation in enquiries and conclusions, and then as obtaining the release of those condemned. It was clear that any influence he exercised was directed to mercy and forbearance.

For some time, the Pope had been anxious that bishops were neglecting their responsibility to preach, and he now had the opportunity to be forthright in his criticism. The Council directed them to appoint those who were capable of announcing God's word and taking the Gospel to the pagans who, as St Paul says, "share the same inheritance, are parts of the same Body, and have received the same promise in Jesus Christ through the Gospel" (*Eph* 3:5-6). It seemed an ideal time to ask for papal confirmation of a religious congregation of Friars Preachers that seemed providentially designed to meet the Council's wishes for the Church and God's People throughout the world at large, and not just for a single diocese.

At first Innocent hesitated for fear that multiple forms of religious life and diversity of Rules might lead to confusion. Furthermore, the idea of a worldwide Order under one head might be an innovation too far, especially as it meant giving an untried group the episcopal prerogative to preach. However, he eventually issued a Bull of Approval, but stipulated that a Rule already sanctioned by the Church should be adopted, and statutes for the new Order drawn up and submitted to him for approval. Now that his followers were about to become respectable religious with a Rule, and the fact that the Pope obviously shared his vision of worldwide activity, Dominic was understandably concerned that they were so few in number, but reassurance was at hand.

We know that he had long since given up going to bed, spent most of the night in contemplating Our Lord and, if rest became essential, he simply lay down on the floor.

One night as he prayed alone in St Peter's Basilica, the Prince of the Apostles himself and St Paul appeared to him. Peter gave him a staff and Paul a book of the Gospels. They told him, "Go and preach; you have been chosen by the Lord." When Dominic pointed out the present shortage of personnel, the Apostles gave him sight of his brethren setting out in pairs to preach the name of the Lord all over the world. A painting of this moment by Hyacinth Beson OP is in the Chapter Room of St Sixtus Convent in Rome.

The Rule is chosen

Dominic returned to Toulouse and consulted with his eighteen, pioneering brethren who deserve to have their names recorded: Brothers Matthew of France; Bertrand of Garigua; Peter Seila, Thomas and William Raymund of Toulouse; Dominic the Little, Michael Fabra, and his own brother Mannes of Spain; John of Navarre; Laurence of England; Stephen of Metz; Oderic of Normandy; William Claret of Pamiers; Peter of Madrid; Gomez, Michael Uzero, Vitalis, and Noel the Prior of Prouille. They selected the Rule of St Augustine, the oldest and least detailed of Western Rules, that offered general spiritual guidance for the common life, and provided an ideal base for the additional constitutions designed for the office of preaching with the commitment to poverty, prayer and study. The community also took the decision "to hold no possessions lest the office of preaching should be impeded by the care of temporal things, and only to receive such revenues as would provide the necessaries of life."

To keep the apostolic spirit vibrant, Dominic found ideal constitutional expansion in the statutes of St Norbert's Premonstratensian Canons as they related to the observance of silence, requesting the superior's permission to speak, fasting and abstinence, the wearing of woollen clothes instead of linen, and the practice of rigorous poverty. He also underlined the importance of chastity and obedience, the observance of the rule of cloister, and fidelity to the recitation of the Divine Office in choir, so that it was said, "he first made the Friars monks separated from the world to enter it effectively." He associated the active ministry with the aspirations and values of traditional monastic life and, in the years to come, would realign behaviour and correct anyone who faltered in religious observance, but always so lovingly that confidence and relationships were never undermined. "He was a great enthusiast for the Rule but, at the same time, his words were so pleasant that the brethren endured the penance imposed by their loving Father with patience and eagerness" (*Prior Ventura*).

Approval

The Rule and Constitutions were presented to Cardinal
Savelli for the Pope's approval that was forthcoming, and
now, the new Order needed a fixed abode. On 25th
August 1216, Bishop Foulkes and his Canons made
available the Priory and chapel dedicated to St Romanus,
the seventh century bishop of Rouen, and gave Dominic
the title "Prior and Master of the Friars Preachers and his
companions." The title "Master" was particularly
appropriate because what the Friars Preachers needed for
their work not so much the paternal care of an Abbot, but
the direction of a scholar-theologian who inspires
learning so that truth can be demonstrated accurately and
effectively. The community celebrated the Feast of their
adopted father, St Augustine, on 28th August, and John of
Navarre renewed his vows before the Master. This
"beloved disciple" lived to give testimony in Dominic's
process of canonization and said of him, "He made
himself amiable to everyone, rich and poor, Jew and
Gentile, and was loved by all save heretics and enemies
of the Church".

As Director of Preaching, Dominic did not think it
appropriate that he should also be the monastic
superior as well, so to that position the community
elected his close colleague Bertrand of Garrigua. The
religious habit chosen was the black cassock and white

surplice of the Canons Regular similar to that of the Canons of Osma, and this was later modified to the familiar white habit and scapular with a black mantle associated with the "Blackfriars". The bridge in London is a permanent memorial to a shining light of the Church, his extraordinary story, and his monumental achievements.

Continued Papal support

Pope Innocent had died the previous month on July 16th and, two days later, was succeeded by the already supportive Cardinal Savelli who became Pope Honorius III. Though frail and elderly, he was determined to continue his predecessor's programme of reform and use his considerable administrative skills to revive Papal finances. When Dominic visited him, he was relieved to find that the Holy Father shared his conviction of the importance of evangelical missions, and would be an energetic patron of the new Order of Preachers. On 22nd December 1216, Honorius issued the Bull of Confirmation: "Honorius to his dear son Dominic and the brethren who have made or shall make profession of the religious life, health and benediction. Considering that the religious of your Order will be the champions of the faith and the true lights of the world, We confirm your Order and take it under our care and protection." The reception of the Confirmation is the subject of a painting by Leandro Bassano's that is in the church of St John and St Paul in Venice.

Honorius and Dominic knew that the best way to protect the faithful from the misconceptions of heresy was to give them suitable Christian instruction. In January 1217, the Pope wrote to the university of Paris where there was an abundance of theologians and asked for some of them to go and teach in Toulouse. He also told the citizens there that he expected them to give support to the project. The arrival of Lent saw Dominic tirelessly preaching in Rome's many churches and drawing large and appreciative congregations. His biographers say he did not forget to visit the hermits and anchorites, was so popular that people cut pieces off his habit as a memory of his being with them, and that he attracted a flow of vocations to the Order.

The Wider Mission: God gives the increase

As he passed through territories on his way back to
Prouille, Dominic saw that military action was having
little impact on heresy. Also, he had been given a vision
that Simon de Montfort would soon die in battle, and
Count Raymond, arch-protector of heretics, would return
in triumph to Toulouse. If these events transpired, as
indeed they did, the position of his Friars and the
seconded Parisian theologians could become untenable.
He met with the brethren on 13th August 1217, and the
brave decision was taken that they should be dispersed
throughout Europe as the start of their worldwide mission.
To their credit, any surprise they might have felt
evaporated in the spirit of trusting obedience to their
fearless and charismatic Founder. On 15th August, the
Feast of the Assumption, they renewed their vows and set
off: Peter, Michael and Dominic the Little to Spain,
Matthew, Mannes, Michael Fabra, Bertrand, and Oderic to
Paris, with John and Laurence who were to complete their
academic studies at the university; Dominic himself and
Stephen to Rome; Peter Seila, Thomas, Noel and William
to remain at Prouille. A happy and timely increase in
numbers came with the arrival of four new members,

Arnold of Toulouse, Romeo of Livia, Poncio of Samatan, and Raymond of Miramont who was destined to succeed Bishop Foulkes in the See of Toulouse.

Scholar-Preachers

Dominic had seen that the Albigensians included trained and cultured members of the clergy and refined women, all of whom were eloquent propagandists. From the experience and depth of his own studies, their value in his encounters with heresy, and his perception of society's individual needs, he knew that his Preachers must receive the best education to ensure the highest efficiency and productivity in the individual and corporate apostolates. Accordingly, he told Mannes, Matthew, and Michael in Paris to open a foundation close to the university that would be an educational resource for members and a likely recruitment centre. The speed at which even his most optimistic hopes were invariably realised is explained only by Divine blessing. By October, the Dean of Saint Quentin and professor of theology, Jean de Barastie, had given the community a house and the church of Saint James that was within the aegis of the university. Matthew, "a learned man ready to meet every point of doctrine", was superior, and Michael director of studies. Within fifteen months the community had grown in number to thirty, some were lecturing in the university and, as John of Navarre pointed out, "everything succeeded as blessed Dominic predicted."

In January 1218, Dominic went to Rome via Milan and Bologna to encourage the Order's growth and acceptability, and he was successful. Within a month, Pope Honorius addressed a series of Bulls to the world's bishops and abbots requiring their universal support "for the friars of the Order of Preachers whose useful ministry and religious life we believe to be pleasing to God." They could now go anywhere in the world and have their work welcomed and encouraged by the ecclesiastical authorities. Now that the university base in Paris was established, Dominic wanted to expand the best opportunities for his brethren's learning and lecturing. He sent Friars Bertrand and John of Navarre to Bologna, where the greatest university in Europe was located, to study Canon Law and open a house. Pope Honorius supported them with letters of approval and, shortly after their arrival, the church of Santa Maria della Mascarella was put at their disposal, an auspicious start to a fruitful venture that would see the recruitment of university professors to the Order.

Developments in Spain

Towards the end of 1218, Dominic asked the brilliant Friar Reginald of Orleans to represent him in Rome, and left for Spain with Michael Uzero and Dominic the Little. They called at Bologna, Fanjeaux, Toulouse to open a priory and convent, and Prouille from where he sent two of the community to open a house in Lyons. They reached Segovia in time for Christmas, and he opened the Order's first Spanish Priory before turning south to Madrid. There he provided a convent similar to that in Prouille, though without the support of Friars and therefore the poorer. He received the Sisters' profession of religious vows and, when he wrote to them hater, he revealed fatherly concern and encouragement in an appraisal of religious life. "We rejoice and thank God that he has seen fit to favour you with this holy calling and to free you from the corruption of the world. Fight the ancient foe of the human race by means of fasting, my daughters; remember that only those who have fought will reach the crown. My wish is that in the cloistered places of the refectory, dormitory and chapel, silence shall be kept, and that in every other thing, the Rule (of St Augustine) shall be properly observed… Since we can give you no financial aid, you are exempt from giving hospitality to friars, or any other persons. Our very dear brother, your chaplain Brother Mannes has spared no pains to bring you to this high state and will take steps to secure its continuance, your holy and religious life." Before leaving his homeland, he presided at the opening of another convent associated with his alma mater, the University of Palencia, and also a house of the Order in Barcelona at the invitation of the Bishop.

A small miracle

On his way back to Rome in the spring of 1219, he called
at the priories and convents in Toulouse and Prouille
before setting out for Paris accompanied by Bertrand. One
night, they stopped at the Marian shrine and sanctuary of
Rocamadour, and in the morning they met a group of
German pilgrims who treated them so kindly that they felt
embarrassed at being unable to reciprocate. They prayed
for the ability to understand and speak German so that
they could, at least, talk to their fellow travellers about
Our Lord. To the pilgrims' initial surprise, they conversed
intelligibly with them in their own language during the
rest of the journey. Before they reached Paris Dominic
told Bertrand to say nothing until after his death because
"if the brethren know about this miracle they will think us
saints, when we are sinners."

More houses open

Dominic stayed in Paris during June and July, organising
a further dispersal of the brethren to open houses in
Limoges, Reims, Metz, Poitiers and Orleans. He asked
Friar Suerio to return to his native Portugal and, within
months, a team was teaching successfully in the diocese
of Coimbra. He encouraged everyone to continue the
pursuit of learning, and sensitively reassured the earliest
disciples who felt embarrassed in the company of fellow

Friars who were graduates and professors. As a former merchant, Peter Seila who was due to go to Limoges, felt uneasy in the company of academic brethren with their volumes on philosophy and Scripture when he had only the 'Homilies of St Gregory'! Dominic told him, "Go, my son, go in all confidence. Twice a day you shall be with me in my prayers. Do not fail me, for you will win many souls and be of much profit." The words were true and Peter established a centre of Dominican excellence.

Return to Italy

St Sixtus: a new convent

Pope Innocent had planned to restore the Roman church of the Pope and Martyr St Sixtus and open a convent there. It was an expensive project and when it was completed, he invited the Gilbertines to take responsibility for the nun's spiritual development because they were experienced in this work. The Gilbertines, a dual order for men who followed the rule of the Austin Canons, and women who followed that of St Benedict, had been founded in 1135 by St Gilbert of Sempringham, Lincolnshire. For reasons that are not entirely clear, they did not find it possible to respond to Innocent's invitation. In July 1219, Dominic left Paris for Bologna where he spent a few months guiding the community's religious development before dispersing members throughout Italy to open new foundations in Bergamo, Asti, Verona, Florence, Brescia and Faenza. He went on to Viterbo where the Papal Court was temporarily located because of disturbances in Rome. Honorius explained he was keen to implement his predecessor's plan for St Sixtus, but the Gilbertines had not acknowledged his reminders. He asked Dominic if he would take charge, and also use the opportunity to open the first Dominican Priory in Rome's Appian Way. This suggestion may have been initiated by Cardinal Ugolino da Segna who had become the Order's helpful and admiring friend in Rome.

In the course of nurturing the convent of St Sixtus, Dominic found that some of the Roman communities of nuns were not in a spiritually healthy condition, mainly because many parents deposited daughters in convents rather than incur the expense of a marriage dowry. Consequently, the rule of enclosure was ignored, and the visits of friends, relatives, even admiring suitors gave an atmosphere more of a social club than a centre of religious life. Dominic talked to Honorius about this and the Pope asked him to restore monastic discipline in the convents, a sensitive task he accomplished in a relatively short time much to the Holy Father's satisfaction.

The Second Order

Dominic had always valued women religious and their capabilities, but his foundations at Prouille, Toulouse and Madrid did not actually belong to the Order of Preachers. With the help of Cardinal Ugolino and the noble lady Diana d'Andalo who persuaded her grandfather to transfer ownership of the church of St Nicholas, he was able to open the first Convent of the Order's Sisters in Bologna, once again with St Augustine's Rule and appropriate constitutions. Pope Honorius approved this extension of

the Order of Preachers to women who would be known as
the Second Order of St Dominic or Domincanesses. They
followed strict observance of the cloister, were devoted to
long hours of prayer and, though initially contemplative,
would later involve themselves in the education of girls.
One distinguished Sister is St Agnes of Montepulciano
who died in 1317, and whose Feast is 20th April.

The first General Chapter

Pope Honorius next gave the Preachers the church of San
Eusorgio in Milan, authorised a new foundation in Viterbo,
sent letters of thanks to everyone who had helped the Friars
in any way, and conferred the title "Master General" on the
Founder. Dominic then wrote to the foundations calling the
Order's first General Chapter to begin at Pentecost, 20th May
1220. Paris, Bologna, Toulouse, Segovia probably
participated as the centres from which the Order was
spreading, but there is no certainty about representation from
other houses. He was conscious of the wonderful
contributions others had made to successful development, felt
"useless and slack", and thought that if someone more
effective were Master, he might be able to realise his ambition
to be a missionary. The brethren did not accept his offer of
resignation, but he did persuade them that, in future, supreme
authority would rest with the Chapter and not himself.

This first assembly renewed the Order's commitment to

mendicancy and monastic values while accepting that essential journeys would require sensible dispensation, though whatever food and bedding was offered should be accepted. With regard to approved departures from the Rule and statutes, the guiding principle was that "the order has been founded for the sake of preaching and the salvation of souls, and zeal should be directed to the goal of being useful to the souls of our neighbours." The place of continuing study pervading the Friar's life and the consequent fulfilment of his vocation was underlined, as were the essentials of the Apostolic life, and the conduct of preachers who, according to the Master, "should always be speaking either with God or about God." It was at this time that the Order decided that its fundamental unit should be the Convent, a group of at least twelve led by a Prior, with or without a house or church of their own. Each would appoint a Professor to reflect the teaching responsibility of the Convent as a place where students were educated, and that gave doctrinal support to the area it served. The result of this particular decision would be extended because, in 1221, when the Bishop of Metz, for example, asked for a convent to be opened in his city, he specified that it would provide not only "preaching for the laity but also lectures for the (diocesan) clergy."

Preaching in Lombardy

When the Chapter closed, Dominic made a brief visit to Milan to encourage his Preachers who were dealing with heresy in Lombardy. He suffered a brief illness there with characteristic patience, and returned to Bologna as soon as he was able. In the meantime, the Pope had written to Abbots and Priors asking them to appoint a community representative to join a mission to Lombardy led by Dominic to preach against the heresy, and "proclaim the Word of God so that the light of the truth may lead home those lost in darkness." The intended corporate effort did not materialize, but he took a small group of his own Friars to bring wanderers back to the Church. It is reported that many returned thanks to their preaching and to the miracles that Dominic wrought in God's name, and through his own prayer and penance. There were reports of the sick recovering, sinners repenting, heretics and non-believers converting, and food being multiplied for the benefit of others. He proceeded to visit the convents in Bergamo and Verona, preaching to the people as he went, and never missing the chance to call on any religious community that happened to be on his route.

Rome again: a new community

When he returned to Rome in December 1220, Dominic was disappointed to find that the nuns of Santa Maria in Tempulo who had intended to join the St Sixtus community had changed their minds, but he won them back to their original intention and restored observance of enclosure. On Ash Wednesday, 24th February 1221, the day chosen for the formal opening of St Sixtus, the ceremony was interrupted by a remarkable incident. Napoleone Orsini, the nephew of one of the attending Cardinals, was so injured in a fall that he seemed to be dead, but Dominic's prayers revived him and he quickly made a full recovery. The rearranged opening took place the Sunday following, and a few weeks later some of the nuns from Prouille arrived to strengthen and help with the settling in of the new community. The Friars already in Rome had been blessed with vocations, and increased numbers enabled the opening of a second foundation in Siena.

When the nuns arrived, most of the brethren moved to the larger premises of the basilica of Santa Sabena that Honorius had generously assigned to them with the gift of one of his own properties on the Aventine Hill. A few remained to attend to the spiritual and pastoral needs of the St Sixtus nuns, and Dominic continued to take an interest in their religious formation under St Augustine's Rule and approved constitutions. As always, he preached throughout the city, and as usual visited those who had chosen the life of a religious recluse and grateful for his warm interest and benevolent guidance.

Preaching to pagans

With matters settled at St Sixtus, Dominic was able to give attention to the Pope's Bull to all the Prelates of the universal Church commending him and the Order to them. It encouraged his vision of leading the brethren on an even wider mission that involved collecting religious throughout Europe and directing them to preach to the pagans who lived just beyond the frontiers of Christendom in places like Morocco, Hungary and Armenia. Then, on 6th May 1221, he received a copy of a letter Pope Honorius had sent to King Valdemar of Denmark regarding a proposed Scandinavian mission to Livonia. Again, the Pope commended the Dominicans and made it clear that "in addition to feeding the faithful with the Word of God, they also preach the name of Christ to the Gentiles." Since this was the only document in Dominic's lifetime that associated his Friars with work among the non-believers, it can be assumed that he wanted to lead this particular mission himself. He sent Friar Solomon to Denmark, his native land, with a letter to Archbishop Sunesen expressing the hope that he might soon come to be with some of his Friars on the Livonian expedition.

Further Expansion Planned

From December 1220 to May 1221, Dominic was in the Papal Court making sure that all was well with the Order's future circumstances in relation to the expectations of the Holy See. He returned to Bologna on May 30th to preside at the second General Chapter, due to begin on 2nd June 1221, and the main item on the agenda was the Order's continued expansion. Though obviously blessed by God who gives the increase, it had been more or less random outside France and Italy but now, in the light of the Pope's announcement of its universal involvement, coherent planning of more distant foundations became essential.

Since 1219, he had organized the Order's growth himself, but if he were now to go away, it would mean that Priors of the major houses like Paris, Bologna and Toulouse would have the added responsibility for colonised territories. This was obviously too much for one person, and the solution adopted was the appointment of Provincial Priors who would be distinct from the Prior of the motherhouse. From this, there developed the structure in which Priors and elected delegates would meet in a Provincial chapter that elected a Prior

Provincial and council, and Priors Provincial and delegates would come together in General Chapter with authority to elect the Master-General.

Mission to muslims

It was decided to send Friars to Germany and Scandinavia to strengthen Dominican presence there, and others to establish provinces in Greece, Hungary and England in addition to the existing bases in Spain, Provence, France, Lombardy and Rome. The Scandinavian mission was unique in being identified with the conversion of pagans, but Dominic's wider concern for non-believers was not forgotten. The Friars in Hungary undertook to organise a mission to the Cumans who had attracted his earlier interest, and Friars from Spain went to Morocco to work for the conversion of Muslims.

England

Dominic made the first contact with England in 1216 when he was given the benefice of St Oswald's Church, Nostel in Yorkshire about the time when Pope Honorius approved the Order. He sent Friar Lawrence the Englishman as his vicar there, and this had attracted vocations. In what was to be the last few weeks of his life, he appointed another English Friar and eminent scholastic theologian, Gilbert of Fresney, to take thirteen companions to open the English Province with Gilbert as first Provincial. As soon as the brethren reached Canterbury, they presented themselves to the Archbishop, later Cardinal, Stephen Langton who was also leader of the English baronage. He invited Gilbert to preach, and was so impressed that he became an immediate and active champion of their mission.

The Friars were mindful of the importance Dominic attached to having priories in university towns so that scholarship and doctrine could harmonize to give people an intelligent appreciation of the Faith. From Canterbury they went to Oxford, the one major university as yet without Dominican presence. They arrived on 15th August, the Feast of Our Lady's Assumption, dedicated to her their first oratory on English soil, and immediately opened a priory and schools. Like Archbishop Stephen, the Bishops realised the value of their presence, and the aristocracy with the ruling House of Plantagenet soon appreciated the social benefits of their educational, cultural and doctrinal influence. From Oxford and London, the Province widened to meet the needs of urban areas like Bristol, Norwich and Newcastle and, by the time of the Reformation there were fifty-four houses. Some of these did not survive, but a further eighteen were founded when persecution ceased. The General Chapter of 1256 offers a touching reminder of the Order's relationship with England. It decided, "that in each convent, in the margin of the martyrology, the day after the Feast of St John the Baptist should be added: This day in the county of Toulouse, died worthy to be remembered the noble Earl Simon de Montfort, zealous lover of the Faith and friend of the blessed Dominic. Let the brethren pray for him and for his race which is joined to the Order by so many ties of affection and gratitude."

Mission to Poland

Pioneers to Poland were led by the Polish Friar Jacek whom the Church honours as St Hyacinth of Cracow. He founded five houses there that became centres of learning and preaching in the towns, and provided Dominican missionaries who went north to Gdansk and eastwards along the Vistula. As a first generation Friar, he made an important contribution to the Order's expansion to eastern and northern Europe, and there are indications that he ventured even to Lithuania and Russia. He died on 15th August 1257 and is buried in the Dominican church in Cracow. He was canonised in 1594 by Pope Clement VIII, and his Feast is 17th August.

Task Accomplished: heaven beckons

In June 1221, Dominic visited the Treviso area. While there, he was one day begging for alms, and was so moved by being offered a whole loaf of bread that he went down on his knees to receive it. In mid-July, he went with Prior Ventura and a few Friars to Venice to call on Cardinal Ugolino and discuss the Order's future. Afterwards, he left representatives there to open a new foundation, and returned to Bologna with the Prior. The heat and the journey left him exhausted but, "of indefatigable spirit", he still managed to conduct a detailed conversation with Prior and Bursar about the Order's organisational development. He complained of a severe headache and was obviously far from well. Ventura suggested he excuse himself for once from midnight Matins, go to bed and try to sleep, but to no avail. Out of kindly concern he was quick to give dispensations to his brethren but never to himself and, for a while, he tried to carry on as usual before collapsing. Because he always spent the night praying in the church, he did not have a cell or bed of his own, and these had to be borrowed from Brother Moneta who also provided a change of clothing when his one and only garment became saturated with perspiration. The detachment and poverty of the greatest Friar Preacher in his travelling mission was powerfully revealed.

Dominic knew he was dying and asked if the novices could be brought to him so that he could offer them his final words of encouragement, and when he had done this he made a general confession to Prior Ventura and two other priests. His fever was raging and, to give him relief from the unbearable heat, the brethren took him up to some high ground outside the city near the church of Saint Mary of the Hills. On 6th August, he asked for Prior Ventura and twenty Friars of the community to come and see him, and when they arrived he preached to them a most beautiful sermon, made a general confession, and received the Sacrament of Extreme Unction. He told them that he wanted to be buried in his own church beneath the feet of his brethren. With great difficulty they managed to carry him back to the Bologna convent.

During these last hours, Dominic reflected on the pattern that had emerged from his itinerant life now at Bologna then back to Rome, Provence, Osma, Palencia and finally to Calaruega. He told his brethren of his gratitude to God who "in His mercy has kept me in pure and unstained virginity." He told them that "if you desire this blessed gift, keep away from everything that can conjure up evil, for it is by watchful care in this that one is loved by God and revered by man." In a gentle reassurance that he was not superhuman, he added, "I must admit that I have taken more pleasure in conversation with young women than I have with old." Knowing that the Order's health and apostolate were associated with personal holiness, he asked them to "be eager in your service of God; strengthen and widen this new-born Order; increase your love of God and your keen observance of the Rule. Grow in holiness. My beloved ones, these are the inheritances I leave you as my sons: have charity among you, hold to humility, possess voluntary poverty." He added, "Holy Father, I have accomplished your work with joy. Those you gave me I have kept. Now that my care of them is failing, I give them back again. See, I am coming to you Father in Heaven."

This was when he told them that he would be more useful after death then in life, and asked them to begin the commendations of his soul to God. As they reached the prayer, "Come to help him saints of God, run to meet him angels of the Lord, take his soul and present it in the sight of the Most High", he passed peacefully to the Lord he had served so valiantly and with such distinction. It was six o'clock in the evening of Friday, 6th August and he was 51. The distraught community's initial sadness was inexplicably overtaken by a sense of the radiant joy that Dominic had always emanated. At the moment he died, Prior Guala of Brescia who had been very ill fell asleep and dreamt that he saw a Friar being taken to Heaven by

Our Lord and Our Lady. At the same time, another Friar celebrating Mass at Tivoli was given a vision of Dominic leaving Bologna with two companions. Cardinal Ugolino came to preside over the funeral of his friend. He sealed the wooden coffin that was then interred in the church of St Nicholas of the Vineyard "under the feet of his brethren".

Devotion to Saint Dominic

Miracles attributed "to God and the blessed Dominic" were soon reported widely across Europe including England, and intense popular devotion brought many people to his burial place. This, and the growth of the Bologna community, made it clear by 1228 that a larger church was essential. This meant that something had to be done about Dominic's present resting place that would be exposed to the elements when the church of St Nicholas of the Vineyard was dismantled. Cardinal Ugolino had become Pope Gregory IX the previous year and, although he was now eighty, he was delighted to accede to the community's request, voiced by the now Master-General Jordan of Saxony, to solemnly translate his friend's body to the new church when it was ready. He said that he was as sure of Dominic's sanctity as he was that of St Peter and St Paul. In the evening of 23rd May 1233, the Friars approached the task of opening the tomb and coffin with some trepidation but, as they did so, a wonderful fragrance filled the air, and the translation of the body in its pinewood reliquary to a marble tomb the following day was an occasion of great joy.

The progress of Dominic's cult that had been blossoming since his death was accelerated by a series of miracles that prompted the Bishop, University and citizens of Bologna to request that their hero be raised to the honours of the Altar. The process was short, and left no doubt about the universal affection Dominic inspired. On 3rd July 1234, within the Octave of Saints Peter and Paul, Pope Gregory canonized his friend and paid this tribute. "I knew him as a dedicated follower of the Apostolic way of life, and there is no doubt that in Heaven he shares the glory of the Apostles themselves."

The Bull of canonization says "Dominic grew at once in age and grace, experienced an ineffable delight in the salvation of souls, devoted himself entirely to God's Word, and by its means awoke many thousands to life. As a preacher and leader to the people of God he created a new preaching Order, and strengthened it by evident and authentic miracles. In addition to his deeds of holiness and beautiful character that made his life resplendent and famous, after death he has given health to the sick, speech to the dumb, sight to the blind, hearing to the deaf, strength to the paralysed. All these are sure signs of the more perfect beauty of the soul within." St Dominic's Feast was entered in the Roman Calendar first on August 6th, the day of his death, then moved to 4th August when the Feast of the Transfiguration became a Solemnity for the universal

Church in 1457, and finally settled on August 8th when the Calendar was re-ordered in 1969-70. He is the Patron Saint of Astronomers, the reason for which may be related first to Blessed Joanna's vision of her son accompanied by the black and white dog holding in its mouth a flaming torch that illuminated the world. Then, Bede Jarrett OP refers to Humbert de Roman and Jordan of Saxony in recording that on the occasion of Dominic's Baptism, "his godmother at the font told of her dream in which the child appeared with his forehead lit by a radiant star, the light from which made the whole world resplendent".

St John Baptist De La Salle, 1651-1719, the Founder of the Brothers of the Christian Schools and the Patron of all Teachers, revered St Dominic as the Founder of a great religious order and the inspiration of teachers and preachers. He said it was difficult 'to find words eloquent enough, to praise highly enough his untiring zeal in preaching the glory of God." St John Baptist's special devotion to Dominic and the other great Founders was particularly evident on their Feasts when "he would spend the time in prayer, recollection, thanking God for giving such people to the Church, and asking Him to grant him a share of their spirit."

Biographers offer other edifying observations that indicate the admiration Dominic attracted, and the confidence people had in his intercession. "His life was one tireless effort in God's service and, as he journeyed from place to place, he prayed and preached without ceasing… The penances he practised were so harsh that his brethren feared for his health; he said that 'a man who is ruler of his passions is master of the world'… He had a stern sense of duty that guided his every action but this never hindered his boundless charity that always distinguished between the sin and the sinner… He could not tolerate heresy and worked strenuously to eliminate it because he loved truth and was concerned for peoples' souls. He had conquered himself before trying to reform others and, accordingly, was privileged to show the Lord's power, as when the dissertation he prepared against the heretics at Fanjeaux was thrown three times by his opponents into the fire but failed to ignite; he revived Cardinal Orsini's nephew; and in answer to his prayer, angels bringing bread appeared in the refectory of St Sixtus."

Dominic in Art

He is often depicted holding a lily and accompanied by the black and white dog mentioned earlier that holds a torch in his mouth as illuminator of the truth. This "dog of the Lord", *"Domini canis"* in Latin, is an obvious pun on "Dominicans". An early portrait by an anonymous Sienese artist now hangs in the Fogg Art Museum of Harvard University. A painting by Titian in the Borghese Gallery in Rome shows a face determined yet shining with benevolence. In 1264, a splendid marble sarcophagus in Bologna was built by Nicolas Pisano and Fra Guglielmo, the inscriptions on which gave Fra Angelico the themes for his paintings of events in St Dominic's life that are in Fisole and Florence. Nicolo de Bari, Alphonse Lombardi and Michelangelo made later embellishments.

Dominic and the Rosary

Dominic's love of the Blessed Virgin and his appreciation of prayer are demonstrated by the legend dating from the fifteenth century that he initiated devotion to the Holy Rosary. This is not historically proven, but he did introduce the process of devoting meditations on particular mysteries to each decade. Dante says he was "fast-knit to Christ" through his vivid and intensely personal prayer. In Dominic's mind, prayer was not limited to human activity because it includes the silent contemplation of God's response that is conversation between the soul and God.

The description "Dominican Rosary" is justified because the Friars simplified and standardised a universally treasured prayer in the course of their preaching, and founded Rosary Confraternities. The Dominican Pope St Pius V did much to foster the devotion and instituted the Feast of Our Lady of the Rosary on October 7th to thank her for saving Christendom from the Turks in the decisive battle of Lepanto in 1571.

Traditional prayer

"O holy priest of God and glorious patriarch Saint Dominic, you were the friend, the well-beloved son of the Queen of Heaven, and you worked many miracles by the power of the Holy Rosary. We ask you to have regard to our necessities. Of old, you opened your heart to the miseries of your brothers and sisters and your hands were strong to help them. Now that you are in Heaven, your charity has not diminished, nor has your power waned. Pray for us therefore to the Mother of the Holy Rosary and to her Divine Son, for we have great confidence that through your intercession we shall obtain the favours we so much desire."

Prayer of the Church

"Lord God, you gave Saint Dominic to the Church of his day as a great preacher of your truth. We pray that he will help us in our time by his merits, his teaching and his constant prayer."

From the Office of Readings, August 8th

"It was Dominic's noble character and ardent love for God that made him a chosen vessel of grace. Though determined, he was always compassionate and his happy heart and tranquil soul were reflected in his kindly countenance. Wherever he was, he was a herald of the Gospel in word and deed, affable and friendly yet fervent in prayer and vigil. His conversations were more with or about God and he rarely spoke of other matters, a practice he commended to his brethren.

Dominic's frequent prayer was for a true and efficacious charity for the salvation of souls. He felt that just as Our Saviour had given himself totally for our salvation, only when he had devoted himself to winning souls could he truly be a member of Christ. It was for this reason that he founded the Order of Preachers. He encouraged his Friars to study the Old and New Testaments, and always carried St Matthew's Gospel and St Paul's Letters that he knew almost by heart. Several times he declined the office of bishop, preferring to live in poverty with his brethren." (Adapted from *Sources of the history of the Order of Preachers*)

The 'O lumen' Antiphon in honour of St Dominic

"O Light of the Church; Teacher of Truth; Rose of Patience; Ivory of Chastity; you have freely poured the water of Wisdom; Preacher of Grace unite us to the Blessed."

Hymn in honour of St Dominic

Sound the mighty champion's praises,
Raise the song for him who came
Charged to tell the Gospel tidings
And to spread the Gospel flame;

Boldly set on lordly errand
Suiting well his lordly name.

Treading down this world of evil,
To his daunting task he goes:
Stript of all, he seeks the conflict,
Turned to face Christ's banded foes;
Faith defending, grace sustaining
With the fire that inward glows.

As Saint Dominic's zealous preaching
Helped the Church on earth to grow,
So, through heavenly intercession
Now he aids us here below;
Holy teacher, lead us all to
Christ from whom all blessings flow.

Sing we to the Triune Godhead,
Honour, glory, power and praise;
May he at our Father's pleading
Deign his children's souls to raise,
Cleansed from stain of sin and perfect,
To his reign of endless days.

*(From the 13th Century Dominican Breviary, tr.
J.D.Aylward OP, adapted, J.Robbins FGCM.)*

Saint Dominic's Legacy

Dominican spirituality

"He left his brethren an inheritance, not of earthly money but of heavenly grace. His last wish was that they should have charity, preserve humility, and possess voluntary poverty" (Jean de Mailly).

Dominic founded his religious order of priests and brothers to undertake the ministry of the Word by teaching and preaching. He presented a model of Christian prayer and Apostolic life as it is portrayed in the Gospel and strengthened by a community life in which members support one another so that they effectively bring the Good News to others with profound charity. Community life is nourished by liturgical and contemplative prayer, self denial, the study of God's Word in the Scriptures, devotion to Our Lord's Passion, the Holy Eucharist and His Blessed Mother, and religious poverty that frees members from the cares of ownership so that they can preach in the way Our Lord recommends.

1216-1347: contribution to learning

The Order of Preachers grew to twenty thousand members. Dominic had responded to the intellectual interest of the age evident in the foundation of universities, his followers opened schools, and their theologians and biblical scholars lectured in the universities with brilliant success.

St Albert the Great, 1200-1280, taught the philosophy of Aristotle and is credited with being the first to make him appreciated in Europe. The '*Summa Theologiae*' written by Albert's pupil St Thomas Aquinas, 1225-74, is a synthesis of theology that Popes have commended to all Christians and pointed out the benefits of its careful study to the clergy.

Albert and Thomas used the Dominican model of spirituality to emphasise that holiness comes from union with God through the Incarnate Word by the grace of the Holy Spirit. It is realised in the action of the theological virtues of Faith, Hope and Charity that guide the earthly pilgrimage with the support of the moral virtues. Holiness and the mystical life are there for all the baptised through the power of the Holy Spirit who guides them with His seven gifts to union with God in prayer and service to others. As Dominic says, "To gaze with love on God, and then share what has been seen with others."

Friars Peter of Tarantause and Hugh of St Cher collaborated with Albert and Thomas in demonstrating how science and philosophy harmonizes in a systematic and coherent presentation of the Gospel. It has been mentioned that England welcomed the Friars led by Gilbert de Fresnay as early as 1221, and that they soon won the admiration the people, the bishops and the Court. Half a century later, Friar Robert Kilwardby became Cardinal and Archbishop of Canterbury, 1273 to 1279, and had the joy of seeing Peter of Tarantause became the first Dominican Pope, Blessed Innocent V in 1276, whose fidelity to wearing his Order's white habit introduced his successors to the custom of the white papal cassock. It was only another twenty-five years before another Dominican remembered as Blessed Benedict XI, ascended the papal throne.

St Raymund of Pennafort

Raymund was born in Catalonia in 1180 into a family with royal and privileged connections. He was educated at Barcelona and Bologna were he took doctorates in civil and canon law, was a renowned professor, became archdeacon of Barcelona in 1219, and joined the Dominicans three years later. Although he loved solitude, he was devoted to the apostolate of reconciling heretics, Jews and Moors. Dominic's friend Gregory IX called him to Rome in 1230 and commissioned him to write his '*Book of Decretals*' of Canon Law that remained the official compilation for the next seven centuries until 1917 when it was revised during the papacy of Benedict XV.

Raymund declined the archbishopric of Tarragona but reluctantly accepted election as Master-General in 1238. In that office he revised the Dominican Constitutions and introduced the system of visitations that would help a rapidly growing Order. He resigned in 1240 and retired to Spain from where he encouraged St Thomas Aquinas to write his '*Summa contra Gentes*' ('*The Truth of the Catholic Faith against the Errors of Unbelievers*'). It is said that he gave some assistance to St Peter Nolasco in founding the Mercedarian Order with the aim of redeeming captives from the Moors. He died in Barcelona in 1275 aged ninety-five, was canonized in 1601 by Pope Clement VIII, and the Church celebrates his Feast on 7th January.

1347-1517: reform, art and new world

Blessed Henry Suso, 1295-1366, is the Dominican theologian who made it clear that mystical union with God does nothing to diminish personal identity, and whose '*Little Book of Eternal Wisdom*' is still treasured. At first, the period witnessed some decline in the Order's numbers and some departures from religious discipline, but return to original rigour and commitment was inspired by St Catherine of Siena, 1347-80, and Friar Raymund of Capua, 1330-99, who established reformed houses in many provinces. Under succeeding Masters-General, the presence of the Order strengthened in Poland, Greece and the Holy Land, and vocations to the sisterhood increased significantly. The Order's concern for Church reform, human rights and responsibilities, and civil justice widened its social dimension, but the tradition of outgoing spirituality always remained balanced by the inward contemplation that frees the soul from attachment to things of earth so that it can welcome the interior birth of the Word.

When it became a rule that every cell should have an edifying picture. Fra Angelico, 1400-1455, painted the cells of his Convent and a Crucifix for the Chapter House. His '*Annunciation*' has influenced posterity in its expression of affection, humility and resigned obedience, and has kept Our Lady's memory sacred during times when critics denied the honour that is her due. He has been described by Georgio Vasari as "the painter whose art came from his religion, who wept as he painted the Crucifixion, and prayed as he selected a brush." Coming a little later, Friar Bartolomeo, 1475-1517, is remembered for simplified detail that enhances large forms that are restrained and noble, as in his touching '*Pieta*'. Pope John Paul II canonized Fra Angelico in 1982 and declared him Patron of artists two years later. His Feast is 18th February.

In 1493, shortly after Columbus' epic discovery, Pope Alexander VI divided the world by an imaginary line running north to south just west of the Azores, and stipulated that lands to the east of the line, with Brazil added later, came under Portugal's jurisdiction, and those to the west were assigned to Spain When the first conquistadors sailed to claim new territories, they were accompanied by brave Dominicans, Franciscans and Augustinians who wanted to take the Gospel to an unknown world. The Dominican Republic is so named because a Dominican landed on the island of "San Domingo".

1517 to 1789: Reformation and Trent

The Order's provinces suffered from the Reformation, but the mission to the Americas continued in one direction, and expanded to India, China, the Philippines and Japan in the other. A revival of Thomism, especially in Spain, coincided with the development of teaching on human rights, social justice, and the explanation of the relationship between predestination and free will by Dominican theologians like Francis de Vitoria and Bartolome de la Casas.

In 1545, Pope Paul III convened the Council of Trent that was the victim of postponements and re-assemblies until the Dominican St Pius V ensured the implementation of its decrees, in the formulation of which the Dominicans made a major contribution in co-operation with St Charles Borromeo. The decrees included:

Sin has not destroyed the freedom of the human will.

Human effort must be made in achieving salvation.

Faith and good works are interrelated.

Devotion to the Eucharist is at the centre of Catholic life.

The Holy Mass is sacrificial in character.

The seven Sacraments are of an efficacious nature.

Guidance was given on the role of the ministerial priesthood; devotion to Mary the Mother of God, and the veneration of the saints; the existence of Purgatory; the validity of Indulgences; the authority of the Pope and Bishops. It is a measure of St Pius V's achievement that Trent's resultant spiritual and institutional reform led to an affirmation of Catholic theology and related practice that would nourish the Church for the next four centuries.

In 1724, the Dominican Archbishop of Benevento was elected Pope Benedict XIII. He continued to observe the Dominican Rule after his election, retained pastoral responsibility for his former See, took an active interest in the diocese of Rome, visited the sick and the dying, enlarged existing hospitals, and built new ones. He was the last Pope of the Counter-Reformation, and in his Bull '*Unigenitus*' he relied on St Thomas Aquinas' teaching on grace to correct the Jansenists' viewpoint, and accept their leaders' eventual retraction.

1790 to 1962: Vatican Council II

The French Revolution and the Napoleonic Wars took inevitable toll on the Order's membership until the revival led by Henri Lacordaire, 1802-1861. This distinguished biographer of St Dominic was ordained a priest for the archdiocese of Paris when he was twenty-five, and very quickly became famous for the quality and impact of his preaching in Notre Dame Cathedral. It was after making a retreat in Rome under the direction of Dom Prosper Gueranger of Solesmes, that he joined the Order of Preachers and later, as French Provincial, was largely responsible for reversing the damage caused by the Revolution's suppression.

The Order blossomed in the United States and Canada, there was a marvellous increase in the active Sisterhood, a further revival of Thomism led by Pope Leo XIII in 1879, and its theologians clarified the doctrine of ecumenism, the liturgy, pastoral life and responsibility, and Biblical studies. The Dominican Cardinal Yves Congar who was born in 1904, is regarded as the greatest ecclesiologist of the twentieth century. He gave invaluable advice to the Second Vatican Council, 1962-1965, that "followed in the footsteps of the Council of Trent, setting forth authentic teaching about divine revelation and how it is handed on." The decade following 1966 saw some fall in numbers but the Order continues St Dominic's fruitful mission in eighty-six countries of the world.

Compendium of the Catechism of the Catholic Church

"The *Compendium*, which I now present to the Universal Church, is a faithful and sure synthesis of the *Catechism of the Catholic Church*. It contains, in concise form, all the essential and fundamental elements of the Church's faith, thus constituting, as my Predecessor had wished, a kind of *vademecum*, which allows believers and non-believers alike to behold the entire panorama of the Catholic faith."

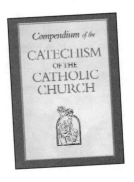

ISBN: 1 86082 376 9

CTS Code: Do 742

Martin de Porres

Martin de Porres is a saint whose popularity has remained undiminished despite his obscure history as a seventeenth century Dominican in South America. His humility and love in the face of racism and prejudice, make him a model for our own time of conflict. In 1962 he became the first South American black saint and patron of inter-racial brotherhood. It was however, his care for the poor, the suffering and even sick animals that made him famous. He performed many miraculous cures in his lifetime and to this day his intercession is sought in many areas with great effect.

ISBN: 1 86082 414 5

CTS Code: B 691

Informative Catholic Reading

We hope that you have enjoyed reading this booklet.

If you would like to find out more about CTS booklets - we'll send you our free information pack and catalogue.

Please send us your details:

Name ....

Address ....

....

....

Postcode ....

Telephone ....

Email ....

Send to: CTS, 40-46 Harleyford Road,
            Vauxhall, London
            SE11 5AY

Tel: 020 7640 0042
Fax: 020 7640 0046
Email: info@cts-online.org.uk

 **CTS**